Unusually Grand Ideas

UNUSUALLY GRAND IDEAS

poems

James Davis May

LOUISIANA STATE UNIVERSITY PRESS | BATON ROUGE

Published by Louisiana State University Press
lsupress.org

LSU Press Paperback Original

DESIGNER: Michelle A. Neustrom
TYPEFACE: Fournier MT Pro

Cover image courtesy Library of Congress,
digitally enhanced by rawpixel.com.

LIBRARY OF CONGRESS CATALOGING-IN-PUBLICATION DATA
Names: May, James Davis, 1982– author.
Title: Unusually grand ideas : poems / James Davis May.
Description: Baton Rouge : Louisiana State University Press, [2023]
Identifiers: LCCN 2022030663 (print) | LCCN 2022030664 (ebook) |
    ISBN 978-0-8071-7659-7 (paperback) | ISBN 978-0-8071-7946-8 (pdf) |
    ISBN 978-0-8071-7945-1 (epub)
Subjects: LCGFT: Poetry.
Classification: LCC PS3613.A9485 U58 2023 (print) | LCC PS3613.A9485
    (ebook) | DDC 811/.6—dc23/eng/20220708
LC record available at https://lccn.loc.gov/2022030663
LC ebook record available at https://lccn.loc.gov/2022030664

For Chelsea and Addie

CONTENTS

I.

II.

III.

I.

Resuscitation

In a hospital classroom, a couple worries
over their plastic baby, its skin, like the walls,
both antiseptic and dingy, worn by the oils
of hapless hands. Eight-months pregnant,

she is more confident than he when pressing
the spring-loaded chest with two fingers
then breathing into the nose and mouth,
making the body swell. He takes his mouth

off the baby's, stares at the potential terror
of this ungodly make-believe, and remembers
his child body heaving inside itself, caught
between trying to swallow and trying to eject

the coin his father told him he should not
put in his mouth because this would happen,
and how the father who was not listened to
heard the mortal silence of the boy's open mouth

and lifted then hugged him with the force
of punishment, which threw the coin
from the throat to the living room floor,
where it played the brief music of his brief death,

of which his father said nothing, the boy having learned
that this life would kill him. And now the small body
of the imagined child in front of him forever dying
and hungry for breath he should not have but gives.

A Species Stands Beyond

For Claudia Emerson & in memoriam

Crouching behind my daughter, I study the bones from her perspective.
Brown and polished, they ascend like wooden banisters.

These two skeletons belonged to tyrannosaurs,
one the same set that transfixed me as a boy,
though its Godzilla posture has been revised

to something more avian and accurate.

The exhibit has been renovated too,
the grand marble hall replaced by habitat and circumstance:

the T. rexes snarling over a duck-billed's carcass,
which, if a recent theory holds, they would not have killed.
They were scavengers, large vultures with huge skulls, tiny arms,

and no wings.

But I prefer the story I learned,
that they were predators, fierce and—I thought this way—evil.

So for my favorite I chose triceratops, the tanklike herbivore
capable of fighting back, its skeleton in the old exhibit
planted like a righteous boulder at the predator's foot.
As if admiring virtue would make me virtuous.

I'm thinking of my friend who died this week.

Gracious, industrious, if anyone deserved to live,

it was she,
and yet, as my wife points out, everyone in our pantheon of enemies—
her ex-husband, our racist neighbor, and the pigheaded colleague
whose only talent is bullying—

still breathes and laughs.

It feels like an accumulation of evidence
that proves something that doesn't need evidence:
a design without design. And Good, Evil, and Fate
are the words of an extinct tongue
that don't appear anywhere on these placards,
while triceratops stands camouflaged in the corner

                                              by Cretaceous flora

in a deromanticized existence.

We move further through the old world, my daughter pointing,
asking for the name of every skeleton, and each time
I'm more confident when I say that I don't know.

Portuguese Man-of-War

I don't imagine pain, but I do feel
a sadness watching it throb on the sand
like a blanket with a mouse inside. Mauve,
shriveled, it reminds me of the birthday balloon
my daughter wouldn't let me throw away,
how it sank each day for weeks,
weighed to the floor by its own weight,
or rather its failure to transcend that weight.
Something of blown glass to this shape,
or something neural—a brain and its nerves,
and only that, what it might be like

to be a mind without a body,
instead of a body without a mind,
which may be the case right now for the poet
who's been in a coma for days and will die soon.
Maybe the mind just drifts away,
like these animals that drift with the weather
and the tide, the tide and time that shred them
as they reach the shore. Look at this one,
its sail translucent, its inky tentacles
taut as a line of verse. After the thing dies,
they go on, stinging whatever touches them.

The Mail

The dogs would hear his truck before we did—
that four-cylinder engine that had to be loud
because it was so weak,

and if the garbagemen set your cans
within ten feet of the mailbox
or you parked your car on the curb
in a way that would require him to reverse,
you wouldn't get your mail,

or, maybe, if he was either angry enough
or not angry enough (we were never sure which)
he'd deliver it and just run over the cans
or nick your bumper with his truck,

and if you were new to the neighborhood,
he'd sketch a map on the back of a postage-due slip,
showing you where you could and couldn't park
and where you could and couldn't place the trash.

All this stopped when his wife died from cancer
and he killed himself. Our new carrier apologized
when she explained why we hadn't received deliveries for days,

and we thought of those maps—
those instructions for how things should be
and how mad he was when they weren't.

Red in Tooth and Claw

Even on the night my friend died
                                    after a long illness—
I won't use the word
                    battle,
                                but the cancer was gone
and then it came back, like some slasher-film killer—

even on that night, the feral cat, the one
that's white and fluffy and sometimes affectionate,
still crossed our driveway, quietly,
from our neighbor's pines to our rhododendrons,

even on that night, she would look for some rodent
or bird to terrorize and mangle
                                    and maybe fully kill.

And I, drinking and grieving on our deck,
was appalled by the world and its gross refusal
to stop being the world,
                            and then embarrassed
not just by my own naivety (though there's plenty of that)
but by my innate human sickness that believes
we matter,
                that someone is listening,
that civility isn't just something we imagined
and don't really follow anyway.
                                That night
I wanted everything to be better than it is,

so I went to the fridge, got out the milk,
and poured it into a little bowl, which I left on the porch
and found empty the next morning.

Spam from the Dead

And two months after the cancer finally ate through
the last tissues that separated him from death,
I get a message from his email address
urging me to click on a link I know I shouldn't,

though I'm tempted, I really am,
to see where it takes me, to see if ghosts
haunt the Internet the way we half hope
they haunt our lives—
                      that is, kindly,
reassuringly.

                  Reassuringly because
if they exist after death, maybe, just maybe
we will too.

                  But I know better
and don't click on anything,

though after I delete it, I search for
and read the last real message he sent:

            dear jim,

            i'm back home now. thank you for letting me visit.

            please tell everyone else I was glad to meet them—

            and let me know if I can do anything in the future.

Tumult and Peace

There was the summer storm, remnants of a hurricane
that exhausted itself over the Appalachians
but still had the strength to cataract the windows
                    of our nine-passenger Estate Wagon,

and eight of us in the car, six siblings and our parents—
my father not stopping on our way back from Toronto,
though we could feel the wind heave against the heavy doors.

But I liked watching the window,
and fear wasn't a word I used for that memory until today
as I drove my daughter home from school in an early spring storm,
rain interrupting the highway
                        like static cutting through a TV show,
dissolving the thin guardrail overlooking the mountain ridge,
with semis behind us, just as blind.

In the calmness after today's storm, I thought of that other storm
and that calmness my father constructed in its midst,
and how nothing kills our gods
                    quite like understanding.

When driving, my father seemed bodiless, a force
that led us, a loud voice rebuking my brothers,
and occasionally, rarely, a hand
                        that would reach back to pat my leg,
as if to say hello, as if to say that he wanted me to know
that he knew I was there.

The Brain on the Table

Boston University's Chronic Traumatic Encephalopathy Center

The slices of brain set in neat rows
look almost like a tray of cookies
the neuropathologists are inspecting for doneness.

Really, though, they've cross-sectioned it
to see how much tissue dissolved
while the man it belonged to was still alive.

This degeneration, the theory goes,
can be caused by blunt force trauma,
the sort football players endure,

and is in part why this particular brain—
and what word do we use here: *Allowed?*
Told? Permitted? Ordered?—the man to murder

another man, as if evil grew in the brain's crevices
like mold, or that violence gave birth
to more violence. That question of whether

an abused child will abuse his child. I remember
the father my father yelled at in the rink parking lot
for punching his kid. The game was over,

the man drunk and big, the kid, like me,
twelve, and my father, weakened
by the last year's heart attack and the stroke

his body was planning, capable only of yelling,
Look at yourself! before calling the cops
who may or may not have done something.

One image shows parts of the brain melted
from the inside, leaving two rough triangles
of emptiness, their sharpest angles on top,

like a sinister jack-o'-lantern's scowl,
the kind I carve every Halloween
and put next to my daughter's pumpkin

with its happy face. She always asks
why mine's so scary. Isn't this the idea
that started the tradition? The hope

that we could ward off evil if we just knew
what it looked like and could make it stop
just long enough to look at itself?

At Mercier Orchards

That first creeping-in of fall in August
like a decision that's been made
but not yet been put into effect. An endlessness
to the sky. High winds that rattle the tall
tulip trees. Hold their leaves up closely,
and you'll see a browning at the edges
as though they're burning slowly. The man
picking blueberries with his family thinks
alternately of the mass shooting
earlier that morning at a nightclub,
which he saw on the news that he turned off
when his four-year-old daughter came into the room,
and also of his friend's presentation
on consciousness, which he understood
about a third of, if he understood
anything at all, and he left feeling
both dumber and smarter for having attended.
There's never not an I, the argument went,
in our understanding, and God, whether
we believe in Him or Her or It or not,
is our invention, making us all atheists
because we believe in ourselves
more than we believe in anything else.
So the border of every model includes us
and what we imagine. Try putting something
outside the box and you've just drawn another box.
Like one of those Russian nesting dolls.
More obscure, though, is his understanding
of the gunman. He knows he's absurd
for not understanding how someone can kill
in a world that can produce blueberries;
he can't imagine that the sweetness of it all
could be overpowered—that it
could be resisted for anything else like hate,

injustice, self-loathing, sadness. That's on him.
A failure to think beyond himself.
And the children pick the berries, eating
most of them but saving a few—most are ripe,
some have begun to ferment. And this is his
favorite time of year and he is happy,
under the endless blue sky that is not endless.

God Is Crying Again

                                —sobbing really,
a sheen of snot across His face,
redness spread over His forehead
like a polluted sunset, His hands trying
to wring the sadness from His eyes.
He's just a child, perpetually learning
what disappointment is
and that He's responsible for it.
He wants so badly to be good!
But then we show Him what He's done.

Here is a man, cradling his wife's purse
as he walks out of the hospital
in which she died. Show God the purse
filled with the particulars of the life
He failed, the wallet, the tissues,
the lipstick, the pen, the cough drops
in thin wax paper that remind Him
of yellow flowers about to open,
and He cries. He wails when we tell Him
about how the man must drive home,
open the door to an empty house
still fragrant with the love that's been lost.
Mention flies probing the eyes
of the hungry who plead for His mercy,
or bring up the film of rubble dust
on the girl pulled from her shelled house—
God weeps some more, then tosses
a divine blanket over His head.

The problem is that what's eternal
cannot grow older or wiser as we do,
so He remains just a child who needs
gentle patience and the affirmation

of so many odes, hymns, and prayers.
So light your candles. He wants to know
that He's a good boy, He wants to know
how happy He's made us and that
we will always love Him, even when
He's done something wrong.

The Mending Wall

The Frost Farm, Derry, New Hampshire

No one noticed as I left both the tour group
and the path to follow the wall, the woods
  growing thicker, the wall itself crumbling,
stones scattered like blocks on a child's floor—
  there was order, but barely, which told me
these stones were the ones I wanted,
  obscure enough, I thought, to be authentic.
Blistered over with lichen, the first few
  swarmed with larvae. Then I found one
that was more loaf than ball, an ax-head almost,
  and small enough to fit beneath my shirt,
where it sanded down my skin so my side
  bled slightly as I smuggled it to my car.
And what did I want it for? So it could sit,
  as it does now, here on my desk,
like a paperweight or primal weapon?
  In part, I like it because nothing suggests
it once made something, or rather,
  that it was part of something made,
something actual that became abstracted
  when the homesick poet remembered it
and the farm he sold before moving to England,
  then wrote about them, constructing the wall
in others' minds, in my mind, a thought
  I can touch as though it were concrete proof
of thought itself, weighing roughly
  as much as a handshake. My own neighbor
shook my hand on the porch we shared
  the day she was discharged from the hospital,
bullet fragments still lodged in her brain
  from the night her boyfriend shot her
in the jaw and she drove herself home
  back to the apartment next to mine,

where I found her outside screaming, and held her
   until the ambulance came. We shook hands
weeks later, her neck in a brace, those shards
   permanent sparks in the x-rays of her skull.
After the paramedics took her away—
   it was hours past midnight and so quiet—
I wondered what my responsibilities were,
   and still do. Who knows if the stone is real,
if the poet ever touched it. She said, "Thanks,
   neighbor," because she didn't know my name.

Ed Smith

Instead of deer or turkey in the yard,
this morning we find Ed Smith,
or a man who says he's Ed Smith.
Elderly, dressed in a khaki jacket and pants
with a white Polo tucked partially into his belt,
he sits beside me now on our deck
while inside my wife calls the sheriff
to see if anyone is looking for him. No one is.
He knows nothing except the name,
not even how he got here or why
he would be walking at all just after sunrise.
I ask him if he saw the cows in the meadow
along the roadside and he says no,
that he didn't come that way, but I know
it's the only way he could have come.
I ask him if he's married and he says no,
then maybe, and I catch myself
manufacturing a sort of condescending pity,
condescending in the way that all pity is,
thinking of him as a body with no self,
a ghost in reverse, an orphaned memory
of someone else's grandfather now lost
and unaware that no one knows who he is,
including himself. In the old stories,
the dead forget themselves and walk witless
through the underworld like boats
adrift and pilotless, and maybe that's why
we invented the self or the soul or the spirit,
some indelible quiddity that cannot die,
because this, to be forgotten by everyone,
even our own minds, seemed—and is—
inexcusable, the worst sort of indignity.
But maybe this spell will break, and the hero
will return, however briefly, to talk with the sheriff

who'd otherwise be bored this Sunday
in a county where nothing happens
except for things like this. Maybe a wife
will be found, or a son or a daughter,
who will laugh when picking him up, the laugh
the acceptance of what cannot be changed.
So my wife and I wait for that someone
who will know what to do, leaving Ed Smith
to sit quietly in our chair, without questions,
his hand tapping his knee to the rhythm
of a song that he's remembered or imagined
and isn't there but seems to be beautiful.

Ruby-Throated

I've seen dogs guard rawhide this fiercely,
their hackles raised as defense
becomes its own pleasure, the way

an argument craves itself or a sweet wound
in the mouth keeps calling for the tongue.
And as the summer ends, these tiny birds

become only more violent in their vigil.
One male positions himself in a nearby birch
and waits for invaders to try the feeder,

usually letting the other males drink
a moment before he charges twenty yards
in half a second, too often buzzing me

as I read on the deck. So when one assault
causes me to spill my drink, I pledge
to take the feeder down or at least not to refill it,

sounding like the father yesterday in the park
who confiscated the ball his boys fought over.
But then my daughter shows me how

occasionally, in between the battles,
a female, her colors muted but no less
beautiful, ascends from an unseen perch

to drink. We watch her lean into and then
away from the feeder's fake yellow flowers
before returning to her hidden branch,

a flight that sounds like a fan or the wind
in a girl's ears as she swings, watching boys
fight over what she'd never want for herself.

Learning to Cry in the Parking Garage

Because my father never showed me how
until I was thirty-five and his mother died
and it was late, too late, to learn from him,
and because he taught me something else
earlier, something dangerous, when he drove himself
and my mother, who let him, to the hospital
for his heart attack where they sawed open his chest
after they put him under—because of all that
and so much else from others and myself,
I've come here, like a hurt dog, or the people
we say are like hurt dogs, to let my body
heave itself into grief as I think about the friend
I've just left who's clearly had a stroke
months ago but still won't see a doctor—
that terrible slurring speech, his half-sunk face
and dilated eyes, and then that feeling
that he's already gone, that this is a beheading
that will last months or years and that we
have to watch it.
             I'm bent double now,
sliding down the concrete wall, feeling
both narcissistic and full of self-loathing, my head
landing in my open palms, as I remember
the others with their cancers, one in hospice,
one unable to eat solid food, my poor,
poor friends—and it's such a stupid thing
to admit that I don't know how to do this,
though my body seems to, just like it knows
how to vomit. Here I am, underground,
in the worst light humans have invented,
the light of mines and warehouses, the air
fetid and damp, where the stains don't decay
and chewing gum turns charcoal-black
under the wheels. So my friends are dying,

just as years ago they were having children
before me, and I climb back into my car
and look for the ticket I'm worried I've lost,
wiping my face with my useless sleeves.

II.

Out Too Far

Home from work, he's taken off his coat,
turned off the light, and lain in bed
alone, as he has done for months,
though it's only five o'clock or so,
and his wife and daughter are downstairs
wondering why he's not with them.
His wife, he'll find out later, is worried
he hates them. How to tell her
that he sometimes doesn't know how
he's ended up in bed? That he's not
sleeping, or even thinking? That he's
gasping, and that's about it, that his day
has been moving toward this moment—
the dark room a piece of driftwood
for an unskilled swimmer who's gone
out too far and pauses to gauge the distance
he knows is likely to kill him? Still,
through that distance he can hear
voices he loves wondering where he is.

Ideation

During the worst days, as I'd slouch on our deck
                            too drained to read or eat

or enjoy the sunlight I told my wife
I was going outside to enjoy,

I'd think about it, about killing myself,
but not with real intention—

just what it would be like, and the imagined belt
would always turn into my brother's hands,

and the abstract weight I carried around
would translate into his knees on my chest

as he choked me, which, when we were kids,
he did many times. I couldn't scream or beg.

It was always his decision whether to keep going,
and he was always too afraid not to stop.

Account

"Are you a danger to yourself?" my wife asked
after I told her I was depressed, that I felt
as though my face were melting from my skull
and that I had to hold a huge medicine ball
as close to too heavy to carry as it could be,
but that it was getting heavier—
and then I recognized the metaphors didn't work,
that language couldn't carry this thing
any better than I could. Was I a danger to myself?
I liked myself less than the dinner I couldn't eat
and would throw away. Still, I paused at the question,
paused each time I heard it from the few I told,
because it made me feel as though I were in a bank
with a stranger who could have been my friend,
except he kept too close, definitely too close,
as I asked the teller for everything in my account,
and she gestured with her eyes toward the button
that trips the silent alarm and calls the police,
but I shook my head and said nothing
except thank you as she handed me the money.

Image Search: "Depression"

A woman with her stiffened hand to her head,
an expression that could mean migraine
or, if this were comedy, which it isn't,
the mock suffering that follows a bad pun.

A teenager sitting in the doorway,
back against the frame, knees cushioning
the arms that cradle the head,
so that her body forms a half-melted W.

A man shouting at his wife, arms raised, as if
signaling a touchdown.
                             None of these correspond
to the way I felt at 4:00 a.m., running
the trail in the pitch-black park, to how
I needed a darkness I'd probably survive
to escape the one I knew I wouldn't.

Pantheon

I loved the yellow poster board
scented with the Elmer's
I used to fix the gods and goddesses
to their names in two traditions
(the Roman always in parentheses),

their figures cut from a workbook
as carefully as anything I had ever done,
then colored with pastels so my togas
and sandals were gaudy, parrotlike.
Zeus with his hand cocked,

palming a lightning bolt, as if
readying a Hail Mary pass. Poseidon
halved by azure ocean. Artemis,
standing on one leg like a heron,
aiming her bow. And there were others

who didn't make it to the board:
the Hesperides, with their apples and siblings
Momus and Oizys—Blame and Woe—
gods my teacher, who wanted me to finish,
said I would have to learn about later.

After Receiving a Scathing Reply to Well-Intentioned Advice Given to a Younger Poet

I thought of Dante's Virgil,
not the steady guide from the *Inferno*,
but the awkward shade in the *Purgatorio*,
the one who, visiting a realm he's been denied,
flusters and stumbles, tries to bribe Cato
with flattery when Cato, having been blessed
with purgatory, wants nothing of it—
the Virgil who eventually disappears
because he isn't needed, and is in fact
an impediment, so he literally goes to hell,
which isn't a happy place at all,
though it is the one that people read about.

A Momentary Stay

Outside my window, the sound of some small slaughter.

It's night, and the woods, not fifteen feet away,
belong to those killers with the keenest eyes:

the coyotes we never see, though we find their hairy scat,
the foxes I have seen playing like dogs, and the owls
that pounce as quietly
                                and suddenly as a stroke.

It could be any one of them ripping the scream
out of an animal I'm also unsure of.
                                      Maybe a raccoon,
maybe a possum, maybe the rabbit we love
to watch eat the low-hanging blackberries.

The scream didn't wake me, though. I was already up
worrying about other fears before this specific terror lit the night.

So I go downstairs, check on my sleeping daughter,
head outside with a flashlight that can only cough a flicker,

and—what else is there to do?—shout at the darkness
that actually seems to listen to my voice
                                   and stops
what will continue later, and elsewhere, without me.

A Note about the Cinderella Pumpkins

For my daughter

We dampened the paper towel just to the point
of its capacity to carry water and still retain its shape.
Then we folded it—"like a letter"—slid it into a freezer bag,
and dotted it with last year's seeds,
finally putting the package here on this desk
that catches the morning light and heats up enough in spring
to make writing here unbearable, which it was that spring,
which almost everything was that spring.
                                        And Addie,
we left that bag alone for more than a week
while we went on vacation, where I—
if you're reading this, you're old enough to know
(if one is ever old enough to know)—
thought quite seriously about wanting to die,
even though everywhere I looked, people, especially you,
were joyful—it was Disney World, after all.

Forgive me, Love, my difficulties with joy,
which I've always found puzzling. Drunkenness,
yes, I understand that. Happiness, sometimes.
But the way you smiled at the princess as she greeted you,
the bounce in your knees, all seemed a foreign language
I wanted to learn but couldn't.
                                        When we returned,
the bag, clouded like a greenhouse, swelled with vines,
some still half in seeds like baby cartoon chicks
wearing parts of their shells. We planted them
near the souvenir fairy house you adorned with flowers
and notes to welcome the fairies you were sure would show,
notes you found the next day answered in tiny,
tiny script and sprinkled with purple glitter,

concrete proof of what you've always known:
that there *is* magic. You inspected while I
watched on, not sure how much longer you'd believe
that I, like you, was excited and convinced.

Depression in Saint-Méloir-des-Ondes

The donkey my daughter loves
cannot reach the flowers that grow
in the film of soil the ocean breeze
has lifted to the roof of the barn.

We don't know what they're called
and speak too little of the language
to ask the farmhand their name,
though we can tell they're delicious

by the way the donkey cocks its head
to two o'clock toward the roof
and strains its prehensile lips
to almost reach them, an effort

that looks like remembering
a word you can almost recall,
how it nearly touches the voice—
"It's on the tip of my tongue," we say.

And I don't know what to say
to myself, or the man I become,
inside those days and nights of hurt
I cannot argue my way out of.

I know it won't be enough to say,
"Remember the orchard over there,
its plums and cherries, and apples
just forming from the blooms."

Not enough to remember the tides
we hear beyond the meadow, how
they leave the beach cracked
like ancient porcelain. Not enough

to repeat the Auden lines I muttered
to myself last night at the restaurant
when I felt the depression coming on,
eerie as a suspicion of being watched.

"The lights must never go out,"
I said, "the music must always play."
And it almost worked: the intoxication
of asking for and receiving the tray

of oysters gleaming like an ornate clock,
then the bouquet of mussels,
and the baked sea bream symmetrical
as a well-wrapped Christmas gift.

But I've learned that you can love
pleasure and still want to die
while absolutely not wanting to die,
a situation that requires, if nothing else,

some patience, the precise gentleness
the donkey grants my daughter's hand
as she offers the wanted flowers
to the mouth that craves and destroys them.

Unusually Grand Ideas

Besides the standard catalog of side effects—
weight loss, insomnia, dry mouth, dizziness,
   etc.—the label lists "unusually grand ideas,"
and it isn't long until you have them. First,
   the idea of the morning, when the cardinal you hate
for its murderous and often scatological attacks
   on your car sings and wakes you and you
do not hate being woken or the song and think
   that, yes, it's possible to separate the art
from the artist, and that if it's not, then art
   redeems us the way the vendors of Kraków
redeem the cobblestones on June mornings,
   spraying them down with their hoses,
the night's drunken grime washed away
   in a beautiful moment of mist and steam.
Second, the idea of your own body breathing,
   a good ache in the legs from yesterday's run,
the heart you didn't want to pump still pumping
   to keep the brain you didn't want to think
still thinking, how both of them stayed with you
   like friends you don't deserve, the kind
who endure your most acrid insults
   and coldest silences but still pick up the phone.
Third, not the idea of love, but its presence,
   the woman who held you those painful nights
as closely as she now holds your sleeping daughter
   who fled some nightmare, navigating
the 3 a.m. dark to dive into the warmth of this bed
   and forget those monsters. You remember
those fears, what it's like to stand at the doorway
   of your room before a forest of hissing shadows
that want to eat you, remember the faith

you have to have in your own terror to sprint
through that dark to the only place you know
    will save you when you get there, if you get there,
which you will, you know it, you will, you have to—

Which Do You Value More?

I bought my daughter a Venus flytrap for five dollars
   at the orchid nursery in Florida City, where the orchids
  hang from the ceiling and crowd the shelves, striking
as the paper lanterns that float like jellyfish in the skies of Chiang Mai.
   Reds and oranges, violets and pinks—extravagance
  is the word, as if nature, tired of the dreary camouflage it designed

for dust-gray mourning doves and brown toads, said,
   This next round is just for me. Some art is indulgent,
  and that's why it's good. Compared to those
pastel and neon flowers, the stunted flytrap looked as though
   one of last year's flowers died in a pot that hadn't yet received
  a new flower, so some strange grass with teeth took advantage of the vacancy

and, unassumingly, set up shop. But it's what she wanted,
   and on the ride home she told me how Venus flytraps
  don't just eat flies—they chomp down on raw hamburger too!
That's what the book she read that made her fall in love
   with the plant before she ever saw one told her.
  I knew about the hamburger, though I didn't tell her,

because when I was a boy, I read the same book
   and also convinced my parents to buy me a flytrap,
  and I even successfully lobbied for the raw hamburger
which I took to my room and dropped into the dinosaur jaws
   I didn't know people thought looked like labia, and watched
  as the burger fell out—it was like feeding a nearly invalid grandfather

who doesn't want to eat, when really what I expected
   was the velocity of an alligator's ravenous snap.
  Better to have the world disappoint her than her father,
I thought. And when we got her plant home and put it
   on the table and picked out a little raw meat, I was surprised
  that it did close, not as fast as a gator's mouth, but fast,

automatically, sort of like the way her hand closed
            around her mother's right after birth, an instinctual grasping
        that fascinates us because it seems like will, it seems like love,
and maybe it is, but it's not conscious of itself. And who says
            love has to be conscious of itself? Which do you value more:
        planned gestures like the giving of roses and chocolate or visceral action,

your lover shielding you with his or her body
            when you both mistake the transformer blowing up
        for a bomb—a move that says *I'll die for you, darling,*
without even thinking about it? We hold onto what we love
            the way almost-falling people hold onto railings.
        I'll take the grasping every time. It's what my body meant

when I held onto my wife as I cried and cried and didn't know why—
            well, I knew I was depressed, but the pain had no source.
        I felt like a poorly shot bear in those awful minutes after the bullet,
how it doesn't know where the threat came from and thinks,
            maybe, that the trees did it, or the ground, but it still looks
        for something to hide from so that thing doesn't continue to kill it.

I held onto her and cried until we were kissing
            and then making love. Did things get better after that?
        A little, and then they got worse, and then better, and then worse,
and then better, and then worse, but that's life, right?
            The point is that this time the plant took the food
        because sometimes the world doesn't disappoint us.

Why I Didn't Tell You I Was Depressed
and Needed Help

Because I was the youngest child for so long
and almost never got to play the video games
my brothers and sisters did, and because
instead I'd watch the pixelated plumber
dodge the crab-walk attack of grimacing mushrooms,
detonate red brick with his raised fist,
bound from floating wall to floating wall,
and time his jump just right to land on the pipe
where a fanged plant rose up and down
with the regular rhythm of our lawn's sprinkler.

Because when our hero did die, cut down
by a rotating bar of flame or clobbered
when a helmeted turtle heaved a hammer at him,
he'd jump, sort of, with his arms raised
in what looked like a shrug, and his face,
at least to me, didn't appear upset,
and the music didn't sound upset either,
but whoever was responsible for his movements
would usually curse and throw the controller
so hard it rebounded when the cord ran its length.

Because then sometimes my brother
would punch a wall, and sometimes he'd punch me,
even though I never made a sound as he played,
never, and because then I would cry quietly,
holding a tissue to my bleeding nose and watch
as the game restarted. Which is to say:
it took me a long time to understand emotion
wasn't always as obvious as a rash or a sneeze,
and that the only time I could pick up the controller
was after everyone else had left the room.

First Compost

Of course it stinks, this garbage can
fashioned into a kind of enlarged
digestive system into which we throw
our scraps and leftover leftovers,
where they melt slowly into a slurry
even the raccoons won't touch.

I churn the slop with a shovel,
excavating the crocodile skins
of avocados and their stubborn,
woody hearts, the mango peels
in their last days as mango peels,
a baguette rioting with mold.

All that sustained us this summer
when I couldn't sustain myself.
"I just want to die," I'd mutter
to the midnight shadows, and wonder
how long I could continue
the conversation. Here's a corn cob.

Here are the grubs whose chewing
we hear from the porch and call
"Satan's choir dining on an unholy salad."
At the bottom, the soil they've made.
I lift it to the top, touch it, can see
finally that it may be useful someday.

Hot Sex

They've finished lunch and gone upstairs
where they begin making love, the tender
but urgent sex of a married couple
with an empty house for an afternoon.
They kiss, and he caresses her, but soon
she breaks off her soft song of pleasure
to say *That's hot,* which he takes as keep going,
but really what she means is that it's hot
as in burning, and then she asks him,
resigned panic in her voice, *Did you
slice one of those serranos into the guac?*
He did, he tells her, and then he realizes
the implications, tripping over his apologies,
but she tells him that stopping
makes it worse and pulls him closer
so they're joined and he feels it too
until they move fast enough, it seems,
to outrun the pain, and they're laughing
between breaths and moans—laughing at the pain
they know will be there when they stop.

On the Last Night of the Summer I Wanted to Die

I spread the blanket over the driveway
that still remembered the afternoon's sun,
and scanned the darkness that the thin light
of our small mountain town could not obscure.
It would be too easy to say it was the falling stars.
Too easy to say it was the thrill of seeing some
seem to come so close they made me flinch,
too easy to say that they brought the realization
that I did not want them, or anything else, to kill me,
though a month earlier I'd sat through a storm alone
hoping the wind would rip off the roof
and take me with it.
                              No, it was what happened
after I went back inside and came out again—
my daughter, still half in the dreams I'd woken her from,
resting against my chest, my wife on the other side,
how we all pointed to each brief, ridiculous splendor
of this unasked-for show, how I loved their laughter,
how I wanted to stay alive to remember it longer.

III.

A Work in Progress

And maybe, he thought as he left the party—
his friends' drunken singing becoming faint,
their voices less distinct with distance—maybe
he wouldn't be so sad if he just accepted the fact
that he would die and then be forgotten,
as would everyone else he loved, and that nothing
he could say or do or think could go against this
ravenous oblivion, making stoic resignation
not only healthy but wise, probably the one way
to score a point in this blowout. Then again,
maybe taking nearly forty years to say this
wasn't so much a triumph as it was pathetic,
his poor, sulky ego finally giving up
its security blanket of vague religious feelings
to wrap himself in the secular fatalism
he loathed but knew was his. So if the Devil appeared
on the dark path he considered taking home,
and, for a little fun, decided to interrogate him,
he would not admit that he once believed poetry
could somehow save him and his loved ones
from nothingness, the way he wouldn't confess
to having liked a band he liked but knew was bad—
that is, he believed it knowing his belief was wrong,
but not any more wrong than his friends
who tried to drink or eat or drug or fuck or pray
their way out of despair. The couple, for example,
he saw kissing in his carport at another party,
one he had hosted a few months back. Maybe
in the thrill of ditching their respective spouses
busy drinking martinis and eating cheese in the kitchen
with the other guests, they had forgotten
he had already left to walk his dog. (Who, after all,
leaves his own party to walk his dog in the dark?)

He watched them from the unlit cul-de-sac,
not wanting to ruin anyone's life that night,
or any night, and hoped they'd stop. Instead
their mouths parted a moment and she laughed,
pulling the man's shirtfront toward her
hard so they'd kiss again. And at this point
a workshop, exasperated, would ask, justifiably,
what this poem's about. "You want to kill yourself,
don't you," one reader might speculate, to which
I'd stutter, "No." Then someone else would ask,
"So what should we make then of the 'dark path'
'the speaker' 'considered taking home'?"
Which would prompt a third to join: "Yeah,
he's leaving his friends to go . . . where?
Into the dark! But why not just say you're empty—
why this sidestepping, metaphoric, anecdotal bullshit?
And can anyone tell me why the Devil's there?"
What I wouldn't say is that I tried to imagine
why anyone would care about private pain,
however acute, when, as I write this, children
are crying because the state has separated them—
children and their parents—and placed them—
children and their parents—in detention units
that many call cages because they look like cages
and are in fact cages; meanwhile, a man in Dallas
or Seattle or D.C. is living the last week of his life
because a police officer will soon shoot him
in what the state will label "an incident"
that will begin when someone, an elderly man
or woman, undoubtedly white, peers through a curtain
of cable news, sees an African American man
walking on the sidewalk, and is unable to think
anything except *he's a threat.* "The state is ill;

therefore, I am ill," my friend Paul wrote
after being diagnosed with the cancer that would kill him.
Or, if I shifted the focus of that sentence a little,
I could write instead *Paul writes,* because the poem
in which his lines appear, as an event in language,
is still happening. So, Paul writes. Whitman writes.
Bishop writes. Claudia writes. All while the state is ill.
All while the state murders and bombs and tortures
and seizes. Now he's so far from the party
he can't hear its joy or see the constellation
of string lights above the lawn. The path *is* dark,
very dark, the sky ridiculously crowded with stars,
and many of his friends have died and he feels
both lonely and selfish—what would the dead
and dying give to have the time he has ahead of him?
And someone might point out that that's just
another way of making himself feel bad, the one thing
he's certain he's good at. The Devil doesn't appear.
But there is a skunk rooting through the grass
for snails, looking, as skunks do, slightly serpentine,
the rising moon announcing her white stripes,
an animal no one will let me turn into a symbol
of terrifying hope, because Robert Lowell
has already done that, and I have to tell you
the couple kept on kissing and I said nothing.

Fishing Again at Thirty-Five

Matt whips his line into a quick cursive
    and darts the fly into the trout's thin mouth,
then pulls it, the fish, out of the stream—
    all this motion seemingly one motion,
fluid as a horse's gallop or snake's strike,
    neither the brain forcing the muscle
nor the muscle failing the brain. The bait
    hardly matters, not as it did when I was young
and used hellgrammites, ugly larvae
    that looked like centipedes with crab claws
for mouths. I'd hook them through the neck,
    a carapace-like collar, and cast them
into the pond where they'd sink in dark water,
    and I'd wait, and they'd wait, for something
I couldn't see or control to choose us,
    or not. Matt hands me the rod, and I flop
the fly near the fish that don't take it.
    Then another cast, and then another.
The water is so clear that I can see
    their indifference and occasional
annoyance. To come back to an art
    I left, to feel again my unskilled hand,
to remember all those poor hellgrammites
    I reeled in, their bodies mangled by small mouths
whose whispered bites I never learned to feel—
    it's good to know that you're not good
at something, or at much, really; good to not
    have caught the fish that's held before you,
slick with freshwater and October sun,
    the brown dots along its skin rhyming
with the rocks, the unattainable colors
    attained. You can't do that. You can't do
anything that well—that's why you praise.

Once on Lake Erie

They put the one who couldn't row at all—
because his shoulder was busted and in a sling—
between the two that could, a sort of fulcrum
like a seesaw's, and it was full-on dark
and they were drunk on boredom and vodka
they stole from parents who trusted them
not to be this dumb. The lake was calm,
the tide was low, the canoe took less water
into its hull than they thought it would
when they first dragged it from under the cabin's
cobwebbed deck and over the muddy rocks.
It's here the one for whom the others row
sees something like a vision, a clarity
he hasn't had before, the water turning black
as they leave the limits of the shore's light,
the stars forming a kind of meaning, he thinks,
that only he can see. In other words,
he sees life as it appears to the young:
as though his friends are rowing him to where
he's meant to be, as though they're extensions
of that power that spins the stars for him
and him alone. Then maybe the moon
elbows past one of the few clouds that night,
or his eyes adjust to the dark, but there
in that slightly leaky boat he really sees
what he really hadn't seen before:
the spiders roosting on their arms like crows
in branches above a sudden flood—
he stands as if to run, not keeping the balance
he was supposed to give, and as he wobbles
the friend in back goes left, the one in front
goes right, like a door across a house shutting
because another one has shut, and the canoe
throws them. The water he breathes in

is cold, and his good arm's flapping can't lift
his body up, but his friends find him
and make a kind of raft of themselves,
and swim him back to land, the canoe lost
or sunk somewhere in the lake. He looks for it
the next day, and then the day after that,
as he paces the shore he won't leave
even if he sees it again, which he won't.

The Defense Rests

He had been thinking all summer about hell,
his damnation in particular, of which he was certain,
but he had been wrong enough in his life
to mistrust even his certainty, just as, often,
he would screw up a meal, burn the garlic
or over season the meat, but wait for his wife's verdict
to confirm or refute his assessment, which,
at that moment, had been that he did not see himself
as an especially generous person, generosity being a virtue
of redemption, something that might save him
if he had it. They were on the porch,
watching their daughter water the garden
she had been growing since March, a hodgepodge
of herbs and annuals. Meanwhile, the season's birds,
done with the tasks of breeding and raising their chicks,
frequented the feeder in the rose of Sharon,
offering a series of metaphors for companionship:
the dim and overly cautious mourning doves
blending in with the ground below, venturing
but in the laziest way, like people who travel
but only to neighboring states. The chickadees
that hatched two eggs in the bird box that spring also visited,
not mourning, it seemed, the hatchling that died
hours after it left the nest, but sounding instead
as though they were bickering about perceived threats.

No, you're not very generous at all, his wife confirmed,
the tone unmistakable, the sort you'd use to agree
with something said that you've always thought
but known was the wrong thing to say, though utterly true,
and it was: she cited a time when they were dating
and he won a box of frozen steaks in a raffle
and kept them for himself, deciding to eat alone
rather than share, even with her. But he remembered

far worse examples: how he prayed for others
to pick up dinner checks, and how he hoped
that flights back to his hometown would be sold out
so he wouldn't have to attend a friend's father's funeral.
And so, he asked her to name some goodness he possessed,
and she said that he was smart and cunning—
but those didn't mean he was good, even if
they were true. Loyalty was the only trait they agreed on,
until he realized his loyalty wasn't unconditional,
as a Homeric catalog of former friends could prove.

So it would be hell, as he had all the other sins
in spades, and coldness, the opposite of generosity,
owned him, while in his daughter, tending to the plants
at that moment, assessing their needs in a way
that seemed advanced for a five-year-old, he saw
an empathetic soul, one who saves box turtles and ladybugs,
and whom he never told about the chickadee hatchling,
which was the size of his thumb. He found it in the lawn
at dusk, so he called his friend, an ornithologist,
and she told him not to interfere. He knew, though,
that it would die, and it did. He could have saved it,
could have placed it in a shoebox for the night. Earth,
he thought, is a cold, cold place, and to be good at all,
even in one way, must be an accomplishment,
as everywhere there are only models for selfishness.
The silent-but-mad race of plant life, its choking out
and blotting out; the goring, neck-snapping, blood-
smearing animal kingdom. The thrashers, dinosaur-like,
stalking insects through the pines. *But more often than not,*
his wife said, *you end up doing the right thing.*
He had an odd combination of ego and self-loathing,
and both kept him from being worse than he was.

The cardinals, meanwhile, weren't even at the feeder—
the female watched from a pine as her mate flitted
to the car in the driveway and attacked, again and again,
the bright but common colors of his reflection in the mirror.

The Snake in the Living Room

Had it been a spider or a rat
or the worm I had hoped it was,
I could have handled it—killed it
or angled it into the moonlight
outside the sliding glass doors.

But once I saw the signature slither
and the tongue flickering
like horror-film lightning, I knew
I needed my wife, though she was sleeping,
though the snake was small,

small enough for the dustpan I tried
but dropped in one final attempt
to overthrow my fear. So Chelsea came
from our darkened bedroom and through
the hall to our living room, naked,

not even wearing her glasses,
and pinched the snake (even the dust
it hid in seemed to weigh it down)
then took it outside. Yes, I thought of Eve
and the story I never believed,

though the suffering it's caused
is real enough. When Chelsea returned
and kissed me and said, *Aren't you glad
I found you,* I was and am—it was,
after all, the truth, and I still know it.

Luck

With his eyes closed and body glued to hers
by sweat, as the last aftershocks of sex
pulse through them, he begins to laugh—
not at the absurd faces he knows he's made;
not at the noises (he says he thinks
he sounds like an elk without knowing
what an elk sounds like); not at the time it's been
since they've last made love, the time it's been
since they've had a chance to; not
at the suddenness, at how the routine
of getting ready for work erupted into this,
or that they are now late and don't care. No,
he's heard himself laugh like this before,
there's a delirium to it, the sort of laugh
that follows a reckoning without tragedy,
a scene in which the bloodthirsty Furies
get nothing for their thirst, the sort of laugh
you'd make when the unlikely card turns over
to save you, and the dealer, realizing he's beat,
scowls, as if to say, *Take your winnings*
—take the happiness you should have lost,
take it all, you lucky bastard, take it all.

Wood Thrush

Audubon put his in a dogwood,
its head arched back singing the song
he couldn't describe in words—

I do not know to what instrumental sounds
I can compare these notes, he writes
in aching Romantic prose.

Each song a three-part structure:
ee-oh-lay, the last part a sort of trick
duet as the bird sings two notes at once.

Field guides call the song *ethereal, haunting,*
and warn that you'll hear the thrush
before you see it, if you see it.

In Breton's *The Song of the Lark,*
a peasant girl has stopped harvesting wheat
to listen in hushed awe to the song

we must imagine by reading her expression
as she listens to the bird
that does not appear in the painting.

Five summers in the Blue Ridge,
and I haven't seen a live wood thrush yet,
though I hear them every April

singing in the grove of dying hemlocks.
Searching for them makes the song
feel as though it's without a source.

"Middle of summer," the haiku would go,
"You can already hear that
the wood thrush is gone."

They look unassumingly drab
in photographs, like small
cinnamon robins. Audubon thought

the last part of their song sounded
like the emotions of a lover . . . doubtful
of the result of all his efforts to please.

So much absence in art: the bird we can't see,
the song we can't describe, the autumn trees
that no longer house the song we miss.

And when the song in the painting ends?
The girl walks toward her work and draws
the sickle blade against the wheat.

XO XO

My daughter nestles next to me on the plane,
eating Skittles, the fragrance of engineered
—maybe imagined is the right word?—citrus
permeating the cabin, which for all
the documented awfulness of artificial flavors,
high-fructose corn syrup, and food coloring,
smells, I have to admit, amazing, and must be
dizzyingly so to my daughter, for whom this flight
is a euphoric experience, flying and magic
being basically the same thing to a seven-year-old,
but she's showing restraint in eating the candies,
one by one—minutes between the bites—
as she plays tic-tac-toe against the computer
built into the seat in front of her, the board
in this version some sort of undersea theme,
a pastel coral reef behind it, where instead of Xs
and Os, the marks are marine animals—
turtles for her, lionfish for the computer—
and she's won about a third of the games,
as has the computer, while the other third
or so have been ties, the game teaching her
something about percentages, I suppose,
or overcoming boredom, which must have been
the inspiration that first called the game into being,
an improvised match played in dirt or sand
with sticks or fingers—she's pressing the screen
with her finger, a callback to those games
played before pencils and ink and paper—
and the inventors of that first game
may also have taken inspiration from—
or for all we know may have inspired—
the level lines of early architecture,
lines and angles that would take centuries
of study to one day produce the grids of cities,

towns, and farms our plane hurtles over
at roughly five hundred miles per hour
and thirty-three thousand seven hundred feet,
flying not, though, in the straight lines
of tic-tac-toe, but slightly curved lines
that follow the contour of the planet
that has suffered much from our species
and its tendency to impose rows and columns
across the terrain and then fight wars
to protect those lines, wars that, early on,
like the football plays my childhood friends
would scheme up in our backyards,
were probably first strategized, again,
in dirt or sand—"You go this way, and if
they go that way like I think they will,
I'll run over here"—our species being capable
of thinking in metaphors—we were the Xs,
they were the Os—but unable to trust
the metaphors completely; otherwise
we wouldn't have wars that kill and maim,
I'd like to think anyway, but instead games
to settle our disputes like tic-tac-toe, or chess,
which is also played on a grid, but, ironically,
while we don't trust the metaphors that much,
we do use them with great efficiency
to protect ourselves from the guilt we'd feel—
surely it would be unbearable—if we pictured
the numbers we use to represent the dead
as the actual dead before us, the missing
limbs, the missing fathers and mothers,
and children would stop us, I think, I hope,
force us to come up with some other way,
but there are limits to what we can imagine
we're imagining, so the numbers are just

numbers, the game just a game, a child's,
one whose strife, Wordsworth writes,
is "too humble to be named in verse,"
though in this case we can see that my child
knows the fish and turtles stand in for Xs
and Os that aren't there, symbols that also mean,
she's learned from the cards she receives
from her grandmother, kisses and hugs
that would be given were they together,
and that gesture alone tells us something
about how much absence makes us ache,
how sometimes the best we can do is give
the suggestion of the thing we can't give,
which, one could argue, is how language works
or doesn't work, depending on your perspective
on this very old problem whose answer
might be that all words, even those in poetry,
are no better than the limelike smell and taste
of the candy my daughter eats, in that
they are a representation of the representation
the mind assembles from sensory experience,
itself a representation, which means they are like,
even very like, but are not, finally, true,
while another way of thinking might be that the words,
the Xs and Os at the end of those letters,
they work enough—that if nothing else,
they make certain we're not bored,
that they make us feel like we're with someone
and maybe even a little happy while we wait.

Moonflowers

Tonight at dusk we linger by the fence
around the garden, watching the wound husks
of moonflowers unclench themselves slowly,
almost too slow for us to see their moving—
you notice only when you look away
and back, until the bloom decides,
or seems to decide, the tease is over,
and throws its petals backward like a sail
in wind, a suddenness about this as though
it screams, almost the way a newborn screams
at pain and want and cold, and I still hear
that cry in the shout across the garden
to say another flower is about to break.
I go to where my daughter stands, flowers
strung along the vine like Christmas lights,
one not yet lit. We praise the world by making
others see what we see. So now she points and feels
what must be pride when the bloom unlocks itself
from itself. And then she turns to look at me.

Fish Rain

It's rare, but it happens:
a waterspout forms near land
and raptures the fish to the sky.

We're not quite sure what happens next.
Well, we know that many die,
that some are shredded by the winds,

that some are frozen into chunks of ice,
and that some, some survive
even after the cyclone stops,

and they exist up there a while.
Maybe they're pummeled
but supported by the currents

in the clouds, the way you keep
a tennis ball in the air
with a single racket—kept up

until they aren't and fall,
and even then some survive
to drown on land. What must it be like

to die after that ascension?
Before, life was so much hunger
and short-lived satisfaction,

but mostly buoyancy
without knowing that word
or any word. Yes, they're stunned,

but surely they know or sense
something is ending,
one eye focused on the ground

the other on the lost sky—
and the water an absence,
a memory they can't remember,

while that human sound of wonder
starts up when they're found
and can't, I imagine, help.

A Field of Sunflowers

I don't want them to be anything
but what they were—
not an audience of minor gods,
not a skyline of spotlights.

Not a crowd of child-drawn faces
or a battalion of showerheads.
Not an anxious jury
or a choir whose song
was too perfect to perceive.

Not a cache of organic road signs.

Not the magnification of a bee's eye
I remember studying in high school biology,
which *is* what they looked like

before my own eyes could focus
and see it was a group of things and not just one thing
that surprised me as I turned the corner.

Easily a thousand flowers
crammed into less than half an acre,
and not a house or barn within a mile.

Not just beauty, then, but its excess,
and no author in sight.

All of that meticulous design and care—
who would give such a gift without the pleasure
of witnessing its acceptance?

I thought about it a long time
as I watched the flowers
that nodded but did not answer.

ACKNOWLEDGMENTS

My thanks to the editors and staff of the following magazines, where the poems listed first appeared, sometimes in a slightly different form: *32 Poems:* "After Receiving a Scathing Reply to Well-Intentioned Advice Given to a Younger Poet" and "Moonflowers"; *Cincinnati Review:* "Ruby-Throated"; *Colorado Review:* "A Field of Sunflowers"; *Georgia Review:* "Account," "A Note about the Cinderella Pumpkins," "Luck," and "The Mail"; *Guernica:* "At Mercier Orchards"; *Phi Kappa Phi Forum:* "Unusually Grand Ideas"; *Pleiades:* "A Species Stands Beyond" and "Resuscitation"; *Plume:* "The Mending Wall"; *Quarterly West:* "Fish Rain" and "A Work in Progress"; *Rattle:* "Red in Tooth and Claw" and "Which Do You Value More?"; *Southern Review:* "Fishing Again at Thirty-Five" and "Portuguese Man-of-War"; *Sugar House Review:* "A Momentary Stay" and "Depression in Saint-Méloir-des-Ondes"; *The Sun:* "Spam from the Dead"; *Tor House:* "On the Last Night of the Summer I Wanted to Die."

"Moonflowers" was reprinted by *American Life in Poetry.*

"Depression in Saint-Méloir-des-Ondes" was reprinted by *Poetry Daily.*

"Wood Thrush" first appeared in *A Literary Field Guide to Southern Appalachia,* edited by Rose McLarney, Laura-Gray Street, and L. L. Gaddy (University of Georgia Press, 2019).

"Ed Smith" received the Poetry Society of America's Cecil Hemley Memorial Award and appears on the foundation's website.

Enormous gratitude to the National Endowment for the Arts for the literature fellowship in creative writing that allowed me to complete this book.

The spirits of lost friends and teachers, whom I miss tremendously, appear in these pages, including Claudia Emerson, Tony Hoagland, Paul Otremba, and Adam Zagajewski.

David Bottoms, Robert Hass, Michael Mark, and Marilyn Nelson, thank you for your insights and suggestions on these poems. Thanks, too, to the Sewanee Writers' Conference and its generous community.

Gratitude to my parents, Kent and Valerie May.

Chelsea Rathburn, you're my first reader and the reason I write. Thank you for rescuing these poems. Thank you for rescuing me.

CPSIA information can be obtained
at www.ICGtesting.com
Printed in the USA
LVHW100043140223
739374LV00004B/382